Karen Donovan

Letters to Boulders

Wet Cement Press

Letters to Boulders ©2025 by Karen Donovan
ISBN 979-8-9918692-7-0

Library of Congress Control Number: 2025946316

Photography by Michael Grinley

Wet Cement Press
1908 Yolo Ave
Berkeley, CA 94707

www.wetcementpress.com

contents

introduction

They say that if you learn the alphabet, the rules of syntax, and the standard vocabulary, you can read the earth like a book. As soon as I realized oh that's what geologists do, my heart flew out of my body and pinned itself to rock. I had already lost it for the earth, early, in the wet New England woods of my childhood, where every fallen log was etched in beetle script, and on ocean beaches, where sand at the water edge rippled just like a mackerel sky. The earth was a message, a signal, a text, and all I wanted was to know what it meant. I was certain the earth could be read, but I thought I had to become a poet to do it. I didn't know I could instead have become a geologist.

splendent luster

My friend says she worried about religious idolatry until someone described Orthodox painted icons to her like this: *imagine your beloved has gone away forever but has left you with a photo to keep.* It is the closest explanation I can give for the year I carried rocks. In handfuls, pocketfuls, armloads, walking back from the cove beach heavier on the earth. *So this is what it feels like to wear Martian gravity boots.* It was not science. It was my mania, pure lust the way a crush consumes your idea of who you are and defines what is now necessary for survival—the other, the other's beauty and utter accessibility. I could take them, so I did. All of them. Sandstone, mudstone, quartz-veined, mica-flecked, feldspar-pinked, rounded chunks of vesicular basalt, clast-studded conglomerate. Solidity, claim, mineral existence. The world without mediation, before and without language. As if I had discovered the motherlode, the planet factory. As if she was making them just for me. As scrap. Ballast. To remember her by.

: a mineral luster of the highest intensity.

greenstone

Which you should always be in the habit to pick up, no matter what else you are carrying. Which I am most likely to have on my person at any particular moment. Which may lie waiting for you at the bottom of that frog pond covered wall to wall with lily pads, not to be confused with an actual frog. Which is set precisely at the geometric center of the known world. Which the alchemist imagined first, before getting distracted by gold, that pedestrian also-ran. Which now belongs to the philosopher. Which was torn off the bedrock before anyone you know was alive. Which is a missing piece of a puzzle all the geologists are trying to put back together. Which only pretends to be asleep. Which is precious enough to be encased in a bank vault protected by armed guards, but luckily no one knows that. Which is verde. Which may have rinsed up at low tide. Which would be considered legal tender were I queen. Which I now offer to you in a spirit of gentleness and humanity notwithstanding the grave forces assembled against such. Which shows it serves as a neutral ambassador or talisman of community. Which indicates its pricelessness. Which fits in the palm of your hand and warms there quickly. Which has observed all and said nothing yet. Which belongs to its own epoch and will outlast everything except our plutonium museums probably. Which is also its own polarity-chronostratigraphic unit. Which is clearly a green stone but may not be greenstone, you tell me. Which does not matter to this ode. Which you could include in an express package to alien intelligences as an indicator of our lost innocence. Which would not require translation.

: a field term for any compact dark-green altered or metamorphosed basic igneous rock that owes its color to chlorite, actinolite, or epidote—see greenschist.

density current

Go on, sink. You may not be as deep as you think. Hypnotized by deliverables, flagellated by calendaring, shallowed from disuse, active disuse, in which you have participated, because let's face it no one pays you for the deeps. Your addiction to paycheck caffeine, paycheck nicotine, paycheck cocaine keeps you strolling these light-flooded waters where you can always see your feet, half-buried in sand and slipper shells. Maybe you've been following the money. Maybe it feels like heaven. Tumbling along a gradient like any other respectable paramecium. Chemotaxis: the aroma sharpens the closer you get to the source. Is that fragrance milkweed? Honeysuckle? But the bees have their own plumblines. To sink, you're going to have to swim out. Close your eyes. Feel vacant weight where your heart used to be, that cloudy, cold, salt-laced stream under there. Reach for it.

: a gravity-induced flow of air in air or of water in water, owing to density differences, e.g. from differences in temperature, salinity, or concentration of suspended particles — see also: salinity current, turbidity current, nuée ardente.

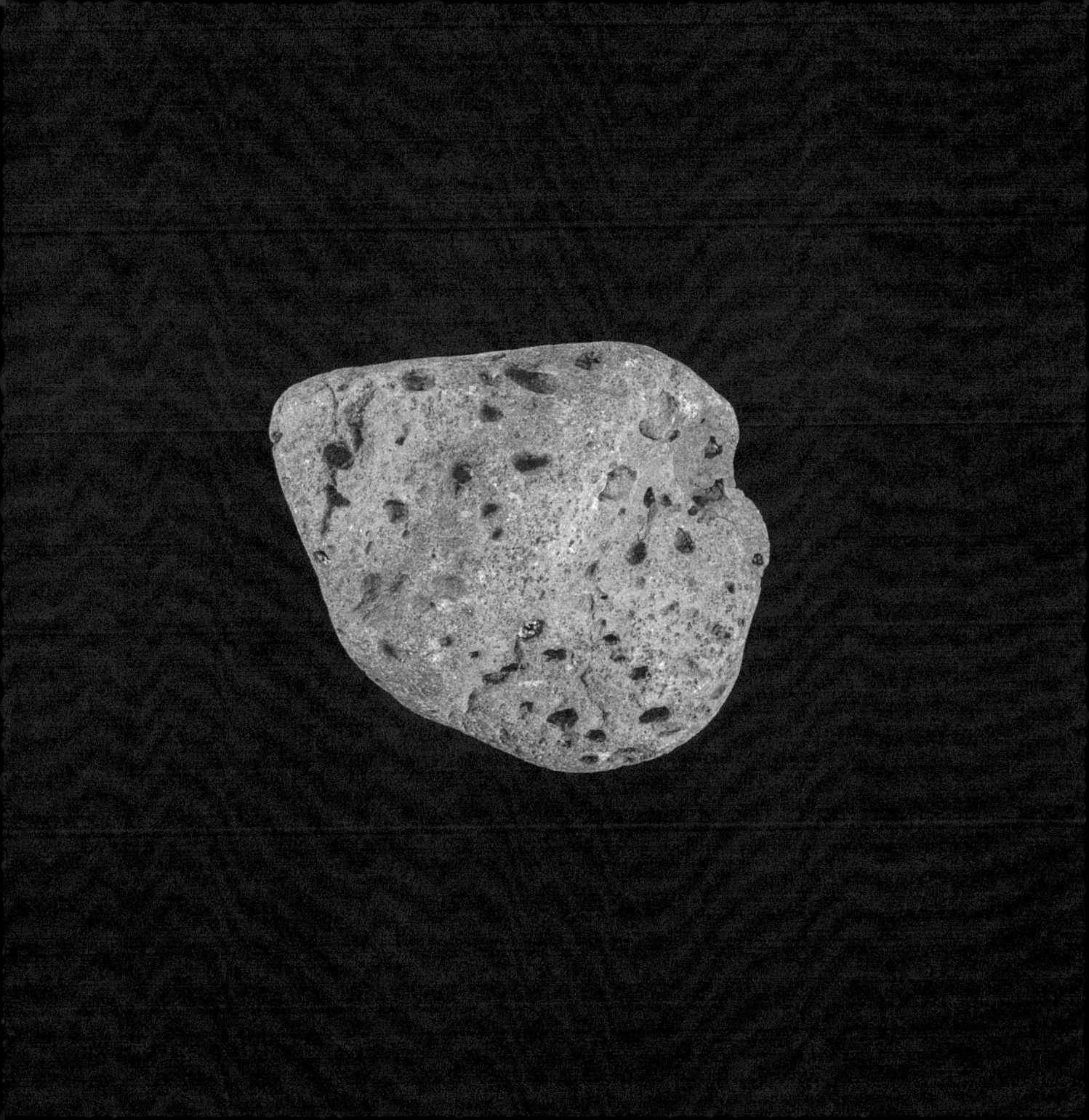

foliation

Apparently this distortion occurs perpendicular to the direction of the principal stress. Which makes sense, since I have indeed felt quite perpendicular lately. As if someone has clicked on my right margin and dragged, what we were always cautioned about in graphic design class: take care not to resize your jpegs the wrong way, i.e., maintain aspect ratio, i.e., don't stretch the picture, numbskull. This time, though, there's no undo. All my crystals have lined up and saluted to the authority of pressure like battalions of toy soldiers standing in perfect rows and columns, obeying the spreadsheet. War footing on the proving ground. But no worries. As if by magic I find myself in shape, ideally muscled for the job ahead, to take the fort, defend the fort, whatever orders filter down and present themselves to my new infantry mentality. Best abs of my life. I thought I couldn't take it anymore, but all I had to do was change. The bones buried down here don't remember what they used to be either.

: a planar arrangement of textural or structural features in any type of rock; esp. the planar structure that results from flattening of the constituent grains of a metamorphic rock.

asteroid

Crossing will take a certain length of measure called *time*. You pay for your passage with whatever you carry, scooped up and salvaged in your last minutes before boarding. Didn't your hand go out in search of something, anything—one precious object to save as if from a flame? Because the world is on fire behind you, a fact you find consoling, what makes the journey necessary to undertake, the impossibility of turning back. Ahead, they say, is too new to name, motion as your geography— rough, rocking, rhythmic music nothing like a lullaby. But soon your hand will loosen and open, and the weight that was in it will fly.

: one of the many small celestial bodies in orbit around the sun.

fissure vein

"I myself consider that in most cases there must have been in the composition of the rock itself some peculiar affinity for the materials held in solution by the percolating waters, which induced, or at least precipitated, a chemical interchange between the two."
—S. F. Emmons, *On the Origin of Fissure Veins*

The crack starts somewhere in your gritty, cemented-together soul. A stress fracture, maybe, like the kind that stings when you run, so you give up running and spend your evenings instead reading everything you can find by Paul Tillich in translation. Or that hairline break in the top of your foot you convince yourself is only a sprained ankle until you wind up in the ER a week later, unable to walk, apologizing to the nurses for your corporeality. But the rift is different. You know exactly when that happened, winter, school morning, eighth grade, clock radio clicking on to the news story about your friend Steve dropping onto the basketball court in mid-dribble, gone down that dark crevasse, they said later, before his head hit the wood floor. And what rose in that instant still fizzes up and solidifies in you as mineral repair, a column of words for why. Not to explain, never to explain, but to fill the space that is always opening and reopening in exactly the same way.

: a type of mineral deposit of veinlike shape, with clearly defined walls rather than extensive host-rock replacement.

subduction

I could help you with that, she says, coming out of the stall and appraising me as I stand before the washbasin mirror, inexpertly trying to straighten my hiked-up miniskirt. We are the only ones in the girls bathroom, and I am milking my hallway pass to avoid French. *You would only need to do a few things.* Blond, compact, a bit shorter than me, wearing all black with safety pins as accessories and exuding the confidence of an eighth grader who has older sisters. Suddenly she is holding a tube of mascara in her hand. Smiling, she advances, drawing the wand out in a majestic gesture as if it were Excalibur. The year is 1970. On the other side of the planet, the Ring of Fire shimmers, shoving massifs of oceanic crust farther down into the recycling trench. At the site of the Kola Superdeep Borehole, the Russians are about to start up a drill aimed at the center of the earth. She does her upper lashes first, then her lower. I watch her, slightly terrified, intensely grateful, completely mute. *Here*, she replies, *you can keep it.*

: the process of one lithospheric plate descending beneath another.

orogeny

I become expert at watching my parents argue. Attack, counterattack, parry, thrust. My mother is willing to be ruthless and unreasonable, so she often has the upper hand. She will accuse my father of never understanding, and he will accuse her of being illogical, and then they'll be off to the races. There is a lot of yelling. From my perspective, they are both right. My mother's anger can be precipitous, rising like a thunderhead of Zeus and striking out at anyone in range who lifts their head, including us kids. As the oldest, I try to keep a low profile but always fail, mainly because my father will come to me for conciliation, holding his hands out, palms up, as if to demonstrate they are empty of blame. Is it despair in his face or cluelessness? Of her indictments he is largely innocent, but that is his fault, being outmatched and believing that logic will ever win the day, especially when she begins to cry. I watch the incompatible truths they defend fold and stretch, reverse, inverse, double back on themselves, grow to cover the sky. They drive at each other like this for years while a hard substance peels off and goes under into the hot netherworld of my own psyche, a melty mix of should haves and never agains, sits down inside me, and refuses to move.

: the process of formation of mountains.

stringer

Truth is, I was decorated a fair amount. When I was a kid swimmer, someone was always hanging a medal from my neck or handing me a garish trophy topped by a tiny metal naiad perched with her knees bent and her arms back, ready to take off. I remember standing on the winner's block with multiple discomforts: cold, wetness, hunger. By the end of the meet, every item I had on was sodden and all I could think about was a hot shower and getting our coach to buy us Big Macs for the ride home. I had my own stopwatch, which I made a lanyard for by braiding those flat strands of green and white gimp, but I hated to wear it because it was heavy and signaled that I was willing to record everyone's splits, which I was not. Later on, I made another lanyard, this time for my lifeguard whistle, my trusty Acme Thunderer, which I deployed summers during high school and college to boss around the members of my town's pool club. The stopwatch and the whistle are long gone, but I still wear a necklace from those days, a gift from my first real boyfriend. It's a small 14K gold heart with my green peridot birthstone fixed at the center, the perfect accessory for every dress-up costumery I have ever owned. Rocko, thank you. The last I heard, you were wrestling alligators. I think of you every time I put it on.

: a mineral veinlet or filament, usually one of many, occurring in a discontinuous subparallel pattern in host rock.

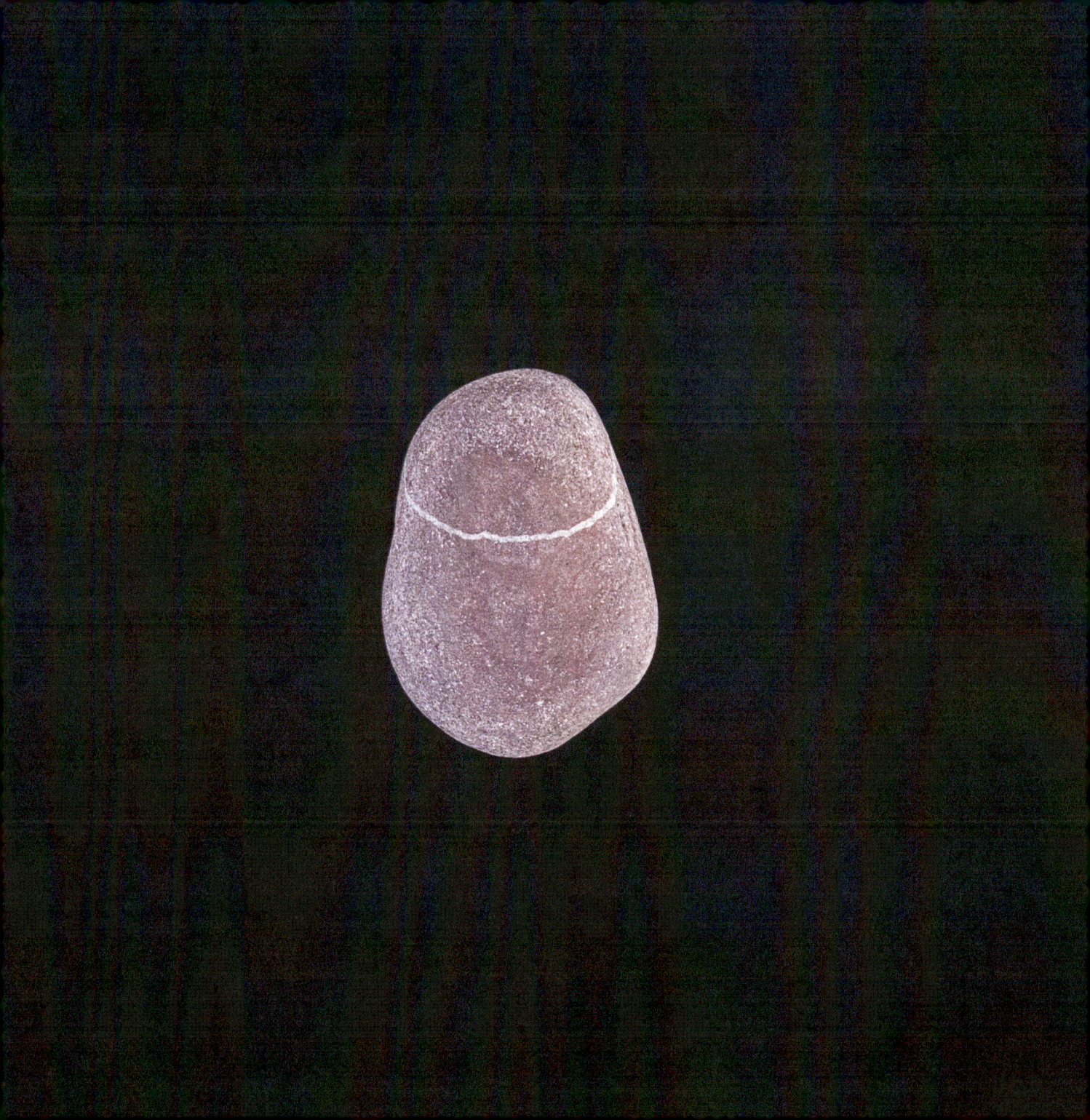

tarn

The night before we climb it, I picture the mountain as a giant-sized barrel chair with a puddle on the seat, Lakes of the Clouds, nearly a mile straight up, above the tree line on Mount Washington. We take the Ammonoosuc Ravine Trail, past Gem Pool, scrambling over the wet stone staircase until there's only rock, lichen, sky, ninety miles of visibility to the west, the rarest of days on this peak: clear, sunny. We sit by the lakes and fall under their cold alpine spell. We throw our heads back and suck in the troposphere, the stratosphere, the ionosphere. We remember the Pleistocene, when all this was buried deep asleep under glaciers while the Laurentide Ice Sheet tucked a slow grinding blanket over North America. Do we smile at each other in the infinite present tense? Chocolate, granola, water from canteens. Perhaps you even kiss me. We know where we have come from but not where we are going. In less than a year, there will be no we. Seventy-five degrees at the trailhead, forty at the top. We're so glad to have these jackets in our packs.

: a small, deep, commonly circular glacial lake occupying a cirque; it is fed by runoff from the surrounding slopes and dammed by a lip of bedrock or by a small moraine.

venus

It's because my eros is panentheistic, I explain to him, not very patiently. Because it spreads across all things, human or not, from the hot gravy inside the planet to every speck of confetti blowing at us in the solar wind. Like, argon to zircon, I add, a little more generously. But he is having none of that. Nope. This is all an excuse, he says, because you had trouble with your mother. I say: it just isn't there, I have no desire to copy myself. And then I think: there's nothing wrong with wanting to love what's already here. The pollen and coatimundi and egrets and mud snails and greenschist and club moss and all the other noble gases. Also, I need to be able to stand on a spit of sand in the dark while the tide runs over my boots. *I am the butter knife of eros,* I think about telling him, *smearing all creatures in naked beauty and connection to everything else.* But I don't say that, thank god. Plus he isn't listening anyway because he has all his own ideas about fertility and child raising, and besides this conversation never happens because we are both too young to know what the hell we are doing, and because I would not have had these words back then, and because even though this is the moment my job description was issued, I never realized I had agreed to the assignment and had already begun it, until now.

: the second planet in the solar system.

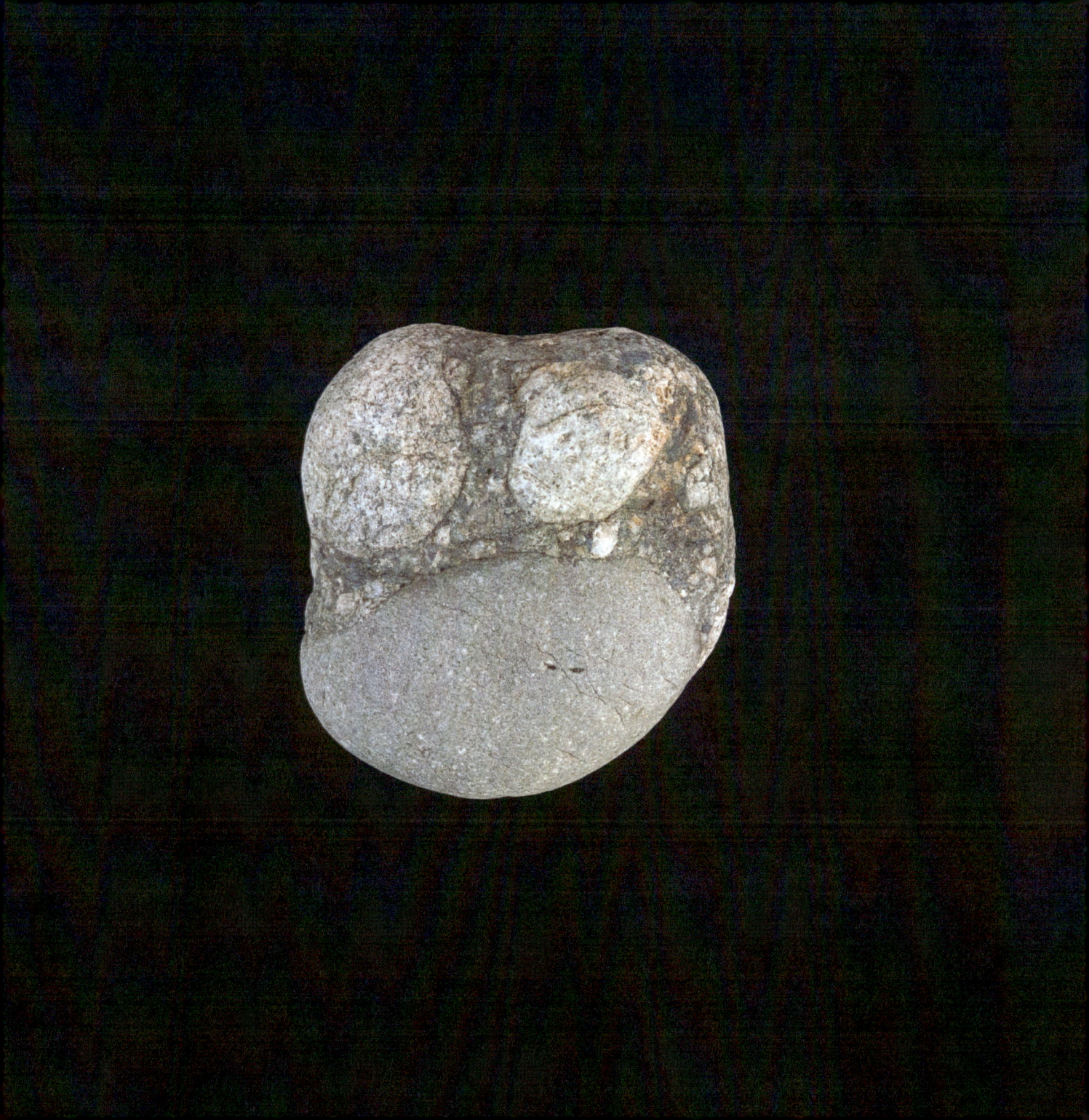

glacier tongue

"Beyond the first impression of cold, the taste was almost exactly what the clarity of the ice implied it might be—clean, refreshing, soft. A feeling of calmness came with it. And then, startled, I realized there was an impression of smell. I breathed in and was immediately taken by a sensation of open sky, clean air, and earth."

—William E. Glassley, *A Wilder Time*

Seven other instances of cold drinks enjoyed while not on an expedition to Greenland: (a) Del's frozen lemonade ritually purchased upon leaving Narragansett Beach before walking back to my car parked on the seawall. (b) A can of grapefruit soda ordered from the counter at Fellini's on Wickenden Street in Providence, along with two hot slices. (c) Iced chai latte at Borealis in Riverside, at an outside table under the sycamores, while watching the bike path parade. (d) Margaritas we had that time on the deck at La Cazuela in Northampton, right before we ordered a meal so killer spicy we couldn't eat it. (e) Raspberry sherbet shake I got at Friendly's on my way home, sunburned as hell, from coaching the swim meet at Look Park while my soon-to-be ex was romancing his newbie on some sailboat. (f) Screwdriver, tequila sunrise, gin and tonic, rum and coke, whiskey sour, experimentally and with great curiosity sampled in that order at a college party before I learned the hard way why you aren't supposed to mix your liquors. (g) First sip of any freshly poured beer, of late this pilsner here.

: a long narrow extension of the lower part of a glacier—see ice tongue.

tephra

Chopper on two hops. Chopper down the line. He fouls one off and it's oh and two. Sinking fast one for a hit. Fastball high. A cutter on the inside corner. Breaking ball in the dirt. A sinker low. Offspeed pitch pulled foul down the third-base line. Swing, popup, first-base side. Breaking ball inside. Fastball outside. Line drive, base hit. Swing and a foul ball off the end of the bat. A ball up and in. A bleeder single that drives in two. A smash right off the scoreboard. Outside ball one. Called strike to the leadoff hitter. Foul to the backstop. Swings and grounds to shallow right. Swing and a miss on a breaking ball down and in. Swing and foul to the right, out of play. Popped up, a towering fly ball. Breaking ball low. Ground ball hit hard to the shortstop. Takes it high, ball one. A strike over the outer half. In there for a strike. Called strike over the inside corner. Inside and low. He takes a sinker, ball one. A curve for a strike over the outer half. Low and away. Rifles a single into center. Fouls the first pitch to the right of the plate and out of play. Line drive base hit down the third-base line. Deep to right and he makes the catch. He gets a piece of it to stay alive.

: a collective term for all clastic materials ejected from a volcano and transported through the air. It includes volcanic dust, ash, cinders, lapilli, scoria, pumice, bombs, and blocks—see also pyroclast.

erratic

The grasses come and go. The clouds, the wind, the soft ones with their searchlight consciousness and thunderous self-possession. I may have slept for some time. A black bird perched for a moment, then was gone. I have been making a song about cattle in a field of green hay and clover and tiny white flowers. The cattle press rivers through the grass as they pass, slowly lifting and placing each hoof and flicking their knotted tails. Then they lower their heads and tear at the grass with their teeth. A quiet ripping sound, like when a girl brushes her hair angrily after being asked too often to yield. There are also swallows in the song, crisscrossing the air above the pasture in vast aeronautical loops. The others have been asleep so long these oracles may no longer matter. But I will speak until they wake and ask me to stop.

: a rock fragment carried by glacial ice, deposited at some distance from the outcrop from which it was derived, and generally resting on bedrock of different lithology—see perched boulder.

shock metamorphism

First trigger warning: we didn't do it, but if our mirror neurons and god-forsaken conscience are functioning, that shouldn't matter. War, slavery, subjugation of peoples, brutality inflicted by the powerful, thievery of the commons, destruction of life in all its forms. We live in history. Our bodies know. Second trigger warning, a partial list of specific topics: beaten by spouse, raped at knifepoint, driven from homes by militias, convicted while innocent, arrested for defending others, molested by a trusted adult, forbidden to speak a native language, kidnapped for ransom, blasted by landmines, murdered in school shootings, sold to human traffickers, abused by caregivers, tortured in secret prisons, robbed of life savings, herded into pens, assassinated and dumped in streets, hungry always hungry, paralyzed by generational trauma, sick with no money for medicine, poisoned by toxic chemicals, et al. Third trigger warning: we assume a shared crisis of spirit. Your soul wound = my soul wound. We will return regularly to the concept of moral injury, with emphasis on the distinction between bystandership and witness. Discussions will be civil, will model open listening, and will be directed toward solutions. Ready set go.

: the changes produced in rocks and minerals by the passage of high-pressure shock waves acting over time intervals ranging from a few microseconds to a fraction of a minute— the only known natural mechanism for producing shock-metamorphic effects is the hypervelocity impact of large meteorites (see astrobleme).

nunatak

Blinded by sun-scoured ice, bedazzled by the nightly bowl of stars that settles around your ears and invites you to join the astronauts, you fall through the hours with yourself for company. Look at your starched white apron smoothed out in every direction to form the ideal circular horizon with you at the center. Note the sun swinging there in hellish consistency every day, except when it doesn't show up at all. Follow the moon's cracked fragments, the whiplashed rose-green aurora driven by your friend the magnetosphere. You have said your piece. You have your memories, frozen like history with the world submerged below. The way your mother cut cooked hotdogs lengthwise and laid them on slices of bread spread with mustard. The way your siblings threw down their towels and raced toward the sea. The way your father spoke your name when he wanted to get your attention. You were always off somewhere else anyway, polishing your skill of sidestepping judgment and befriending trees, who gave you no trouble. So nothing changes. Preachers are still talking about the end of time. Physicians are still seeking the ultimate antivenom. Lovers are still perplexed. O glorious light-drenched monadnock! I'd like to stand here with you in all these feels, but I've got things to do.

: an isolated knob or peak of bedrock that projects prominently above the surface of a glacier and is surrounded by glacier ice, common along the coast of Greenland—from Eskimo, "lonely peak."

conglomerate

Meet the man who loses it all—home, family, friends, job. I can get details. Are town recreation officials giving some youth sports teams preferential treatment? Digging into this. She believed he was her real father until 23andMe indicated otherwise. Exclusive interview to come. Who is stealing eggs from this neighbor's chickens? Following up. Resident claims landlords are conspiring to keep rents high. Think about infographic potential. UFO sighting—need I say more? Not just stealing eggs but also pulling up her peonies. See attached pic she sent me, showing shovel they left behind plus empty beer bottles. Wow, possible DNA retrieval for forensic evidence? When the water rises and the fires come, will we get out in time? Will we have enough insurance? Is the invisible hand of the marketplace still invisible? A street-level opinion poll. Also developing stories: belligerents march, nurses strike, children have had it with school. Police demonstrate force. Mayor instructs us to get out the lifeboats. The powerful do not respond. The best lack all conviction, again. She now reports her shih tzu is missing. I'm on it.

: a coarse-grained clastic sedimentary rock, composed of rounded to subangular fragments larger than 2 mm in diameter (granules, pebbles, cobbles, boulders) set in a fine-grained matrix of sand or silt, and commonly cemented by calcium carbonate, iron oxide, silica, or hardened clay; the consolidated equivalent of gravel.

algal biscuit

Many folks are unaware there is a saltwater alternative to this popular standard. Here follow my preferred recipe ingredients. Three cups all-purpose flour: ponder harvesting, then small-batch roasting and milling, the ripened seeds of *Zostera marina*. You will need official permission to collect them from a protected underwater meadow. You will also need scuba gear. Three tablespoons sugar: if you are nearby to a coast, you could forage for sugar kelp, but I would actually recommend sugar sand. You'll have to find some maple trees. Another good reason to go to Vermont for the weekend. One-half teaspoon salt: you know, the evaporated kind. The pink Himalayan stuff is pretty but will not make a lick of difference to the taste. Four teaspoons baking powder and one-half teaspoon cream of tartar: do *not* substitute baking soda, trust me. Three-quarters cup COLD butter: can be made from a variety of milks, such as seal, sea lion, manatee, dolphin, whale. Churn by hand while practicing gratefulness. One egg: really cool if you can get your hands on a whelk egg case. If not, a skate egg, aka mermaid's purse, will do. Some people use black-market fairy penguin eggs, but this species is endangered, so it is very despicable for them to do that. One cup whole milk: see butter, above.

: any of various hemispherical or disk-shaped calcareous masses, up to 20 cm in diameter, produced in fresh water as a result of precipitation by various blue-green algae.

atmosphere

Onions frying in butter. Garlic in olive oil. Crushed oregano. Aerial effervescence resulting from slicing a very fresh, very crisp green pepper with a very sharp knife. Cucumber. Roasted, caramelized sweet potato. Dill, marjoram, sage, curry. Balsamic vinegar, just a splash. Lemon zest. Thyme. Whole grain mustard added at the last minute. Now you can open your eyes.

: the gaseous envelope surrounding the earth—the atmosphere is very mobile, flowing readily under even a slight pressure gradient; elastic, compressible, capable of unlimited expansion, a poor conductor of heat, but able to transmit vibrations with considerable velocity.

meander scroll

"But perhaps the simplest and yet most dissolvent of all sign systems, the ur-inscription that predated writing and even the spoken word, is the trail itself."

—Robert Moor, *On Trails*

Because evidence of human habitation overcome by undomesticated vegetation is pretty much my favorite thing, finding a pitted cement bridge footing smothered in prickery vines in the wildest corner of the park today was a highlight. Plus the improvised teepee shelter built as a lean-to over an old stone hearth made more visible now through winter trees. (To get there, look for a stand of winged euonymus and turn off the path where it's thickest.) Also because that unholy mess of fur strewn across the meadow, unclear whether deer or rabbit, made me think about a coyote I surprised last night who acted like he was in charge of the library parking lot. So cold, so transparent, this spring welling up under thin plates of ice. Beech grove practicing ultimate silence, candled in pale yellow leaves, every trunk carved eye high with names and dates, hearts and stars. And maybe because how everybody else was inside, watching TV or running the world, any way I went seemed like a big circle back to home.

: one of a series of arcuate ridges and troughs formed along the inner bank of a stream meander as the channel migrated laterally down-valley and toward the outer bank— see oxbow lake.

41

phenocryst

Yeah, finding the only thing that keeps me from full-scale 24/7 doomscrolling is to dig in real dirt. Pull on my overalls, fetch my trowel bucket and long-handled shovel from the basement, go outside, and move earth around. I'll fill in those holes in the lawn, build a new section of garden, plant cosmos seeds saved from last year. Squirrels are interfering with the broccoli, and a groundhog who lives under the shed munches on my zinnias at night. Bring it on. Outside this small eminently undefendable bubble, humans continue to develop effective ways to rip bodies and minds apart and throw their hands up and say *not my fault*. In a cupped palm, the cosmos seeds are impossible slivers, sleeping beings. They lift like paper skeletons and blow away at the slightest breeze, but I'm careful, notch twenty quarter-inch holes in the dirt with my finger, pick each one out of the tangle, drop it in, cover it up, add water, move on to the next. It's a task I can accomplish only while on my knees, bent over as close as possible to the ground. I was just now going to say *we can accomplish* but did not, having no idea if you would agree or could agree and lacking the courage such words these days require.

: one of the relatively large and ordinarily conspicuous crystals of the earliest generation in a porphyritic igneous rock.

world rift system

Check pairs of terms that best describe the Great Separation. Select as many as you wish.

- ☐ Apples vs oranges
- ☐ Beforehand vs afterwards
- ☐ Coke vs Pepsi
- ☐ Digital vs analog
- ☐ East vs West
- ☐ Fate vs free will
- ☐ Good vs evil, etc.
- ☐ Hot vs not so hot
- ☐ Integration vs despair
- ☐ Jack vs Jill vs a pail of water
- ☐ Known knowns vs unknown knowns
- ☐ Lions vs tigers
- ☐ Maybe... vs You go, I don't care
- ☐ Night vs nightlight

- ☐ Old vs auld
- ☐ Paper vs plastic
- ☐ Questions vs answers
- ☐ Regular vs half-caf soy latte no foam
- ☐ Swords vs plowshares
- ☐ Truth vs fiction
- ☐ Us vs them
- ☐ Volume vs mass vs density and why that is so hard to remember
- ☐ Wine vs beer
- ☐ Xylem vs phloem
- ☐ Yankees vs Mets
- ☐ Zero vs the Ten Thousand Things

: a major tectonic element of the earth, consisting of midoceanic ridges and their associated rift valleys, such as those along the Mid-Atlantic Ridge—it is believed to be the locus of extensional splitting and upwelling of magma that has resulted in seafloor spreading.

law of original horizontality

As his body rolled over and over down the hill like a kicked log, the dewy clover pressed underneath flattened and left a dark path behind him. His clothes were soaked. When he reached the bottom of the slope, his momentum slowed and he woke up. Violet was asleep beside him under quilts. Their bedroom was cold, but he was wide awake now from the dream, so he got up, pulled on his robe and a pair of thick socks, and padded out to the kitchen. Moonlight polished the snowy hill outside and poured into the sink, filled with dishes from their late dinner. The bright moon was perfectly round, and as he stood there in his robe and socks, admiring the view, it suddenly winked out, as if a large object had passed between it and the earth. It startled him so much that he woke up. He was in the canoe, floating in the sun amid a patch of water lilies on the far edge of the pond. His line was out, evidently set for perch. He reeled it in through the plants with difficulty, cursing. The bait was long gone. Late afternoon faded on the hillside. Disoriented by the doubled dream and woozy from sleeping too long in the sun, he checked his watch. He had promised Violet a fresh-caught dinner, and it would be late. Annoyed, he took up the paddle and plunged it deeply into the water lilies to wrench the boat out, and as he lost his balance and went over, over and over down into tangled vines, he told himself to relax completely and wait patiently to wake up again.

: waterlaid sediments are deposited in strata that are horizontal or nearly horizontal, and parallel or nearly parallel to the earth's surface.

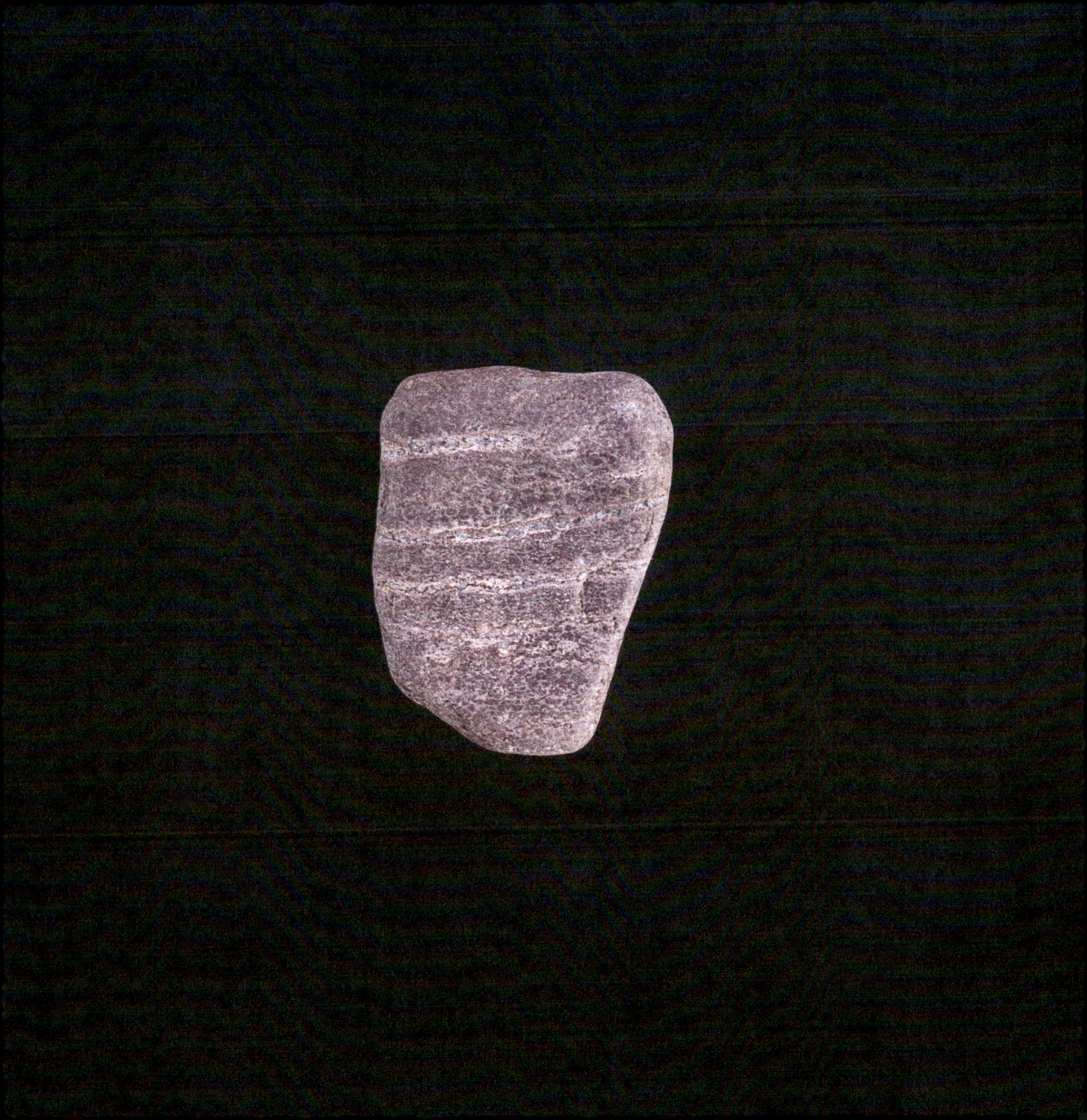

alabaster

A lopsided moon rose over the cove. I paddled halfway out, and except for two men
with flashlights at the boat ramp and a night heron I spooked from the bow of the
Dodecahedron, it was quiet. The men with flashlights were agitated over something,
with each other, or with their small motor launch, and darkness was not helping them
solve their problem. Their voices were low and harried as I glided by without a sound,
and then one of them shouted, "Not yet!" The night heron took flight again with
a vexed croak. The water was covered with floating pads of sea lettuce. On the west
shore, a few cottages still had their back lights on. As a child, I had longed for this
kind of freedom, to be able to slip my kayak into the water at midnight and go out to
watch the moon come up, simply because I wanted to, and to not be subject to the
permission of anyone. Back then, if I managed to escape our house at night, I would
wander the neighborhood, walking through the yards like a visitor from another
planet, seeing all the lives in the lighted windows and enjoying my invisibility.
Occasionally a dog would bark from inside and a human voice would reprimand
it. Even though I knew whose house it was and whose dog it was, everything was
different at that hour. I understood my imprisonment was wrong and I could not
fix it. I understood I would get in trouble with my parents. But my fury lessened the
farther up the street I went. I became another person, almost myself.

*: a compact fine-grained gypsum, white or delicately shaded and often translucent, used
for ornamental vessels, figures, and statuary.*

plate tectonics

Episode 2534 from the great workforce rebellion of 2021 CE: After toiling for more than a year from his tiny kitchen table during a pandemic that kills millions of people worldwide and insidiously and permanently ruins the health of millions more, while taking hardly any vacation days and devoting vast energies to supporting his company's welfare, his supervisor invites him to contemplate how he really should be doing better and emails him a multi-point performance improvement plan for him to sign and then implement within 30 days, or else. This is followed by a compulsory zoom meeting, the purpose of which is to bully him into agreeing with each of the multi-points, a pile-on experience that provokes in him, in turn, shock, shame, adrenaline-fueled embarrassment, anger, incredulity, and an internal bubble of what he will later call cynical hilarity. The mismatch between realities could not be more striking. Within the head and shoulders of his zoom rectangle, he mostly keeps his composure. The rest of his body, outside the frame, blazes with neon resistance at the falsehoods on parade. Like other chronically misunderstood youth who narrowly survive into intact adults, he knows instinctively when he is being inaccurately assessed, and as always it does not inspire him to rise to the occasion. His computer displays, *This meeting ended by host*. Reader, he sleeps on it. Then he walks.

: a theory of global tectonics in which the lithosphere is divided into a number of plates whose pattern of horizontal movement is that of tortionally rigid bodies that interact with one another at their boundaries, causing seismic and tectonic activity along these boundaries—see megatectonics.

granular disintegration

She wants to say something and then reconsiders. Already too much has been said. Words rinse off pages and slide down storm drains to the sea and pop like bubbles out of texts and float in cinders above cities and sublimate out of media files and bind themselves to her skin and coat her lungs and cross the blood-brain barrier and lodge in her synapses, as immortal as microplastics, filling every void and turning the otherwise real into particulate, chumlike soup. The soup is loud. It is gritty and tastes of ink. She wants it gone. Oh, says her friend Phoebe, trying to be helpful, you should do erasures, they're fun. Thought experiment: obliterate conjunctions, leave only punctuation, tweezer away all vowels, blackmail the adverbs. She sees how it will end, in defeat, the combinatorial ferocity of the alphabets defying her ice pick. She surveys her library and knows she will have to burn it. And then the books are history, an infinite, smoking heap. She puts rocks on the shelves. They speak without speaking of a time before and seventy times seven times before. The future is in this music. She holds each one in her hand and listens until she can hear its deep sigh. Like sand sifting a little bit in wind.

: a type of weathering consisting of grain-by-grain breakdown of rock masses composed of discrete mineral crystals, esp. of coarse-grained rocks (such as granite, gneiss, sandstone, and conglomerate), occurring in regions of great temperature extremes.

fireclay

How we will be made, because you foresee the way we will be. Infinite questing, capacity for delusion, intellectual browbeating, carping, drunken midnight debate. How we will hurl our accusations across the tables with the hard force of intercontinental missiles and dress ourselves in treacherous innocence. And because of that innocence, our infectious curiosity, our attachment to the marvelous, you allow also this wonder? How what keeps us so unsure about you also glues us, like barnacles, to everything else you have made.

: a siliceous or aluminous clay capable of withstanding high temperatures without deforming, and useful for the manufacture of refractory products such as crucibles and firebrick.

granite

You want there to be
a baby dragon
inside
but it's probably
just more
feldspar

: a plutonic rock in which quartz makes up 10 to 50 percent of the felsic components and the alkali feldspar/total feldspar ratio is 65 to 90 percent—broadly applied, any holocrystalline quartz-bearing plutonic rock.

earth tide

After the disaster he informs me that nothing will change. I don't want to believe him, but then I do. It doesn't matter what is in our hearts. All the towers will fall. The swells are coming off the seawall at an angle, sending undulating hyperbolic echoes of waves underneath my boat and back out toward the bay. Lift, plunge, pitch, yaw. Lift, plunge, pitch, yaw. *This is strange water*, I think to myself, then say out loud, as if the water is listening.

: the rising and falling of the surface of the solid earth in response to the same forces that produce the tides of the sea.

tremor

I can feel it in there sitting between my shoulder blades, I tell my physical therapist, like weird energy that wants to get out but can't, like a knot of neon light, like an emergency flight plan, a clenched fist, a miniature bus depot bustling with rush-hour commuters, like a runaway buzzsaw, a perpetual-motion somersault, the inhale before a primal scream or a photic sneeze, like a canister of mustard gas and an unpinned hand grenade, like a letter in the mailbox, a tea-kettle whistle, a phantom to-do list, like regret, like premonition, like viruses conferring on where to go next, like glacial advance, almost-petrichor, a spun ticket tumbler, vibration in the rails from an imminent freight train, a particle accelerator, a diamond drill, a frozen mocktail mixing up in the blender, like an egg released from an ovary, a flutter kick, a stutter step, an overfilled quiver, like thermohaline circulation and the deep ocean currents. I can't make it stop. Okay, she says.

: a minor earthquake, esp. a foreshock or an aftershock (see seismic event, temblor).

patterned ground

Second shelf of living room bookcase, left to right, first lines: *[openquote]* Toward the end of 1988, less than a year after the antidepressant drug Prozac was introduced, I had occasion to treat an architect who was suffering from a prolonged bout of melancholy. Despite the flashy, dramatic, and often limelight attention that Nikola Tesla was given in the heyday of his reign in the fields of research and engineering, he maintained a very private personal life. In London, where Southampton Row passes Russell Square, across from the British Museum in Bloomsbury, Leo Szilard waited irritably one gray Depression morning for the stoplight to change. What do the codes used for sending messages back from spacecraft have in common with genes on a molecule of DNA? I am unpacking my library. An acquaintance with Peirce's categorial system is required if his characterization of law as Thirdness is to be understood. Time has always struck people as mysterious: mysterious, in fact, in a number of different ways. In the summer of 1823, my friend _____ entered my study with an air which indicated he had something to communicate. I have tried to keep in mind Proust's cagey and inarguable dictum, that each reader reads only what is within himself. The understanding of Tao is an inner experience in which distinction between subject and object vanishes. Tayo didn't sleep well that night. What in the world are you doing here in the king's hall, Socrates? Matter takes many forms and suffers many changes. *[closequote]*

: a group term for the more or less symmetrical forms such as circles, polygons, nets, steps, and stripes that are characteristic of, but not necessarily confined to, surficial material subject to intensive frost action.

sedimentation

Third shelf of living room bookcase, left to right, first lines: [openquote] The aesthetic dimension of human existence enjoys a curious position in the subject matter of philosophy. The honeybee, living in its beehive, is a social insect. Ideas, like grapes, grow in clusters. Since the mid-1970s, feminist criticisms of science have evolved from a reformist to a revolutionary position, from analyses that offered the possibility of improving the science we have, to calls for a transformation in the very foundations both of science and of the cultures that accord it value. Lord Balfour once said "The great bulk of people infinitely prefer the continuance of a problem which they cannot explain to an explanation which they cannot understand." While speaking of the "crisis in literature" during the 1880's, Mallarmé accused "official prosody" of relying upon "cut and dried rules," an orthodox ever-ready keyboard. Many people say: "Of course, Dr. Ross has seen too many dying patients." It had been like dying, that sliding down the mountain pass. Three years is a long time to leave a letter unanswered, and your letter has been lying without an answer even longer than that. On a fine November day in 1945, late in the afternoon, I was landed on an airstrip in southern Japan. It's May and I've just awakened from a nap, curled against sagebrush the way my dog taught me to sleep—sheltered from wind. A mass of hills of all the colors you can imagine or care to imagine. *[closequote]*

: the process of forming sediment in layers, including the separation of rock particles from the parent material, the transportation of these particles to the site of deposition, the actual deposition or settling, the diagenetic changes occurring in the sediment, and its ultimate consolidation into rock.

sandstone

It's late in the day for sledding at Crescent Park, so everyone sitting in their cars turns on their headlamps. The kids drop into shadow at the bottom of the hill, then hike back up, pulling their sleds over rutted snow toward parents standing at the top. There's a barricade now on the staircase to the beach, with fencing and orange warning tape to keep people off the cracked retaining wall, rebar stays pulling out as the fundament shifts, sixteen thousand years of glacial dunes yielding to the highest tides anyone in town remembers. I walk up Narragansett Ave toward Sabin Point, February, cold wind coming from the north, ice crusts heaped at street corners. From the next house, a clarinet: someone teaching themselves that old Sinatra tune "Strangers in the Night." A few lines of melody, a mistake, a pause, starting over. On the point, the wind is stronger. Two girls huddled at the fishing pier try to light a cigarette. A sign reminds us to recycle our monofilament. Upriver, Providence glows like a circus ring, and downriver past Gaspee the current is emptying in darkness to the bay.

: a clastic sedimentary rock composed of grains of sand size set in a matrix of silt or clay and more or less firmly united by a cementing material (commonly silica, iron oxide, or calcium carbonate); the consolidated equivalent of sand.

accretion hypothesis

"What will outlast us? Concrete, rusting steel, quite a bit of plastic, unidentifiable goop, nuclear waste, sediments with anomalous amounts of phosphorus, nitrogen, mercury, lead, and isotopically light carbon from three centuries of burning fossil fuels that had taken half a billion years to accumulate."

—Marcia Bjornerud, *Reading the Rocks*

Because we could no longer find a way forward, we tried to back out of the maze, undoing our steps and peeling off an item of clothing at every turn, pleading with the ref to stop the clock. *It's not fair, we didn't know, it's too hard, we want to go back.* But once we were naked, we realized there was no way back, and besides no one had been assigned to keep track. So we had to turn around again on the path and stagger through the underbrush of our own discarded clothing, fitting on the hats and coats and boots of strangers as best we could—petticoats and cravats, and bowlers and toques, and goosedown jackets and cutoff shorts, and plaid skirts and tshirts, and pajamas and v-neck sweaters. The more clothing we put on, the more of it lay on the path, tragedies and dilemmas, agonies and immensities, traumas and mythologies of wear. It's too much wear, we yelled at the ref, we want to be naked again. Then the bloodshed began. We had forgotten the past and even our names, but our clothing remembered everything.

: any hypothesis of the origin of the earth which assumes that it has grown from a small nucleus by the gradual addition of solid bodies, such as meteorites, asteroids, or planetesimals, formerly revolving about the sun in independent orbits, but eventually drawn by gravitation to the earth and incorporated with it.

pangaea

It's that story, the old one. The woman, the man. Divided from their origins. In exile due to their suspect character. For expertise at disobedience, let's say. But look here. What makes everyone else follow us through the turnstile, slinking past those cherubim bouncers without a backward look? The forest spreads its limbs over the wall, dropping acorns and pears and catkins. The mosses escape under the door. Geese fly south in the first vee, catfish nose along downstream, moths and mosquitoes flit by, already developing their more annoying tendencies. The bears lumber out at dawn with lunch pails like workmen reporting to construction sites across town. Don't all the exits blow open on that day, and doesn't the whole crew leave together? So why this grief, this nostalgia, this abiding, accursed sense of loss, when the only item remaining in that garden is one small tree, alone, with no one to tend it? No finches to sing from its branches, no squirrels to wring and twist its trunk, no deer to savor its useless windfall fruit, which is delicious but which we only need to taste once, after all, to understand that our real home is elsewhere, is here.

: a supercontinent that existed from about 300 to about 200 million years ago and included most of the continental crust of the earth.

uniformitarianism

Same as it ever was. Friday. Eight a.m. Lace on my boots and I'm off on my regular walk through the neighborhood to Dunkin Donuts to pick up the usual, multigrain bagel and a bottle of coffee milk. Sunny, 65 degrees, mid-December, seems nobody in the northeast needs to wear a coat anymore. Note to self: rake up that last pile of leaves. Past the playground and left on Planet Ave. Christmas inflatables lying deflated on the lawns. Marriage, divorce, birth, death, work, play, illness, health, transporting happiness, corrosive despair, school lunches, giant flat-screens, tiny front-step gardens. Crushed zippo lighter and a lottery ticket in the street. Nuthatch calling. At the counter, Carlee's mom asks her, Will it be a donut or a munchkin? Carlee, quite solid on her feet for a one-year-old, is too busy chewing on her toy cell phone to answer. They decide on vanilla frosted. I have four dollars in my back pocket, and it feels like that's all I will ever need.

: the fundamental principle that geological processes and natural laws now operating to modify the earth's crust have acted in much the same manner and with essentially the same intensity throughout geologic time, and that past geologic events can be explained by forces observable today (the classical concept that "the present is the key to the past") —the doctrine does not imply that all change is at a uniform rate, and does not exclude minor local catastrophes.

graticule

Prime bouldering habitat, this woods, so unlikely in sea-level Rhode Island. At GPS 41.895, -71.43 and elevation 243 feet: Peace Dove and Jesus Loves You lean toward each other where they were dropped by the last glacier onto a flat granite outcrop overlooking Olney Pond. The route up the back of Peace Dove: Warhawk. The back of Jesus Loves You: Jesus Hates You. O you clever climbers, you've named every rock. Improbable and Heart and Egg and Potato and Tomato and Pond Cave and Ship's Prow and Try Again. The boulders are stained with your chalk, cracks and ledges and swales and fissures fingers have gripped, a map to travel, crimp to crimp, where to put a foot next, how far to the next hold. Balance, tension, release—detail solves the problem. The text is hard, an immutable partner crossed with weathered scars and webs of ancient quartz pumped up like the veins of a power lifter. Your bodies are soft. You challenge fixity, change your shape, crouch, roll, hang by one arm. Bucket, gaston, hand jam, pinch, undercling, improvise with the given. I close my eyes, put my hands where you put your hands, conscious of my mind beginning to swarm, my thoughts impatient to be felt for. Turn here like this, yes. Cross over. It's painful, this unbearable joy.

: the network of lines representing meridians of longitude and parallels of latitude on a map or chart, on which the map or chart was drawn—not to be confused with grid.

geologic record

abyssal hill   braided stream   crystal habit
desert varnish   esker fan   forest bed

glacial milk   head wave   inherent ash

joint set   kidney ore   lunate bar
mica book   net slip   oriental amethyst

peacock copper   quaquaversal dip

rock flour   sand flood   thunder egg
updip block   varietal mineral   wrench fault

xerothermic period   young valley   zigzag fold

: the "documents" or "archives" of the history of the earth, represented by bedrock, regolith, and the earth's morphology; the rocks and the accessible solid part of the earth—also, the geologic history based on inferences from this record.

selenology

"Bigger and bigger the planetesimals grew, as the largest swallowed the smaller. Eventually a few dozen big balls of rock, each the size of a small planet, acted as giant vacuum cleaners, sweeping swaths of the Solar System clean of most of its dust and gas as they coalesced and settled into near circular orbital paths."

—Robert M. Hazen, *The Story of Earth*

Enter Theia, theory has it, presumed to be motoring around the new star in the very same plane as baby Earth, just snowballing along like baby Mercury, baby Mars, major-baby Jupiter, etc., blessedly ignorant of the physics bringing it inexorably, whackingly nearer to its destined Newtonian fate: a collision, a smackdown, a pileup involving two fairly squishy, hot objects in the arena of this particular Milky Way tilt-a-whirl, each sporting an attitude and the thinnest gesture of crust laid atop its fizzing scarlet apple magma. It seems the cosmos from the beginning had planned all along to throw these two pies at each other, and that's what it does, as whamoosh all the young rock vaporizes into silicate plasma, and all the elements exchange bodily fluids, and water-balloon-shaped figures rebound through and off, and kerploop something else comes out the other end, something roundish and steaming and swirling, pulled right off our last rib and already cooling and moving away while a hailstorm of condensing stone rains down on us both and a kind of scorched-blue gravity takes over like a staring contest and we are pinned together forever, you and me, by the impact that made us not quite one, not quite two.

: the science of the moon.

fossil

When a quick inventory suggests you have metamorphosed:
- Would rather have manual rolldown car windows
- And dials on the clock radio instead of programmable buttons
- Would prefer long conversations via landline
- Cuts own bangs
- Carries cash
- Has organized life so as to avoid the necessity of wearing high heels
- And possesses zero dresses
- Behaves as though resistance is the best option
- Still believes the personal is political
- Holds strong opinions about punctuation
- Avoids apps
- Shaves not
- Composts

: any remains, trace, or imprint of a plant or animal that has been preserved in the earth's crust since some past geologic or prehistoric time; loosely, any evidence of past life (see also problematic fossil).

mélange

"As fossils and paleomagnetism indicate, there are sediments from continents (sandstones and so forth) and rocks from scattered marine sources (cherts, graywackes, serpentines, gabbros, pillow lavas, and other volcanics) assembled at random in the matrix clay. Caught between the plates in the subduction, many of these things were taken down sixty-five thousand to a hundred thousand feet and spit back up as blue schist."
—John McPhee, *Assembling California*

Partial list of items in a black lacquered box kept on a shelf in my closet: rhinestone money clip holding two folded paper bills, one Honduran lempira, one mil pesos bolivianos, both given to me by my brother after he lost his job with the cruise line; bracelet chain with a smiley-face charm; two starburst brooches; sea glass, various shapes; piece of lead type topped by a lobster dingbat; large green marble; sunflower charm attached to a safety pin; red Christmas bell on a ribbon; orange toy cockroach; tiny blue rubber alien figurine attached to a parachute, one of the strangest gifts I ever got from my mother; toy plane, metal, painted blue; glass earring with scarab pattern; tiny yellow rubber coatimundi; Lincoln penny dated 1979; gold ring inscribed with a K; shell of an Atlantic oyster drill; two matching screw-back earrings with green glass centers; frog clicker; small cat's eye marble; vintage key on gold cord, remnant of a vast hoard collected by a long-dead friend; perfectly oval white stone; horse chestnut seed; Victorian-era shoe buckle with multicolored glass, originally owned by my grandmother, Beryl; steel bolt washer, one-inch, with square center hole.

: a mappable body of rock that includes fragments and blocks of all sizes, both exotic and native, embedded in a fragmented and generally sheared matrix—see chaos.

thermokarst topography

I am late for golden winter sunset light on water but arrive in time to view an orange creamsicle and lavender sky and to read the sentences *You will never touch me again* and *You had no right*, drawn with a sharp stick in the flat wet frozen sand. How are you? someone had asked me earlier, expecting the usual Great! or Busy! or even Hanging in there! followed by an anodyne comment on the weather and how spring was surely on the way, but what I actually said was, Disgusted by the human race, no filters, aren't you glad you asked? Wet sand being so receptive to any sentiment pressed upon it, I imprint my boot soles in a straight line stalking away down the beach from these two messages, thinking *Fucking A* and *You go girl*. Another getaway. No need to take a match to this paper, since the river as the tide rises will make erasure a quick accomplishment, along with all the other headlines from today, including the one about those empty baby strollers lined up like idling taxis on the border of the invaded nation, ready and waiting for whoever might come along and need one.

: an irregular land surface containing cave-in lakes, bogs, caverns, pits, and other small depressions, formed in a permafrost region by the melting of ground ice.

musical sand

After the lecture, I go to the podium and wait my turn to ask. My body is a carillon ringing with desire and hope that feels also desperate, hungry with a dangerous edge. Bells and knives, that's it, the song I am hearing, the song that is inside me. I don't know my question until I say it, and then like a fool, I ask her, But there is a possibility for beauty? Oh, beauty, she answers, and then she smiles. Beauty is necessary and inherent, not contingent, although it can often feel contingent and seemingly fragile, serendipitous, unearned, an unlikely gift, easy to overlook, often overlooked. She pauses and adds, But not by you, am I right? But suffering and brutality, I forge ahead, worrying it. Do they not erase beauty? This may happen, she admits, but beauty returns. But, I say, suffering and brutality also. She sees that I will not let it go. They do return, she says. And then you yourself may choose which you will serve.

: a sounding sand that emits a definite musical note or tone when stirred, trodden on, or otherwise disturbed.

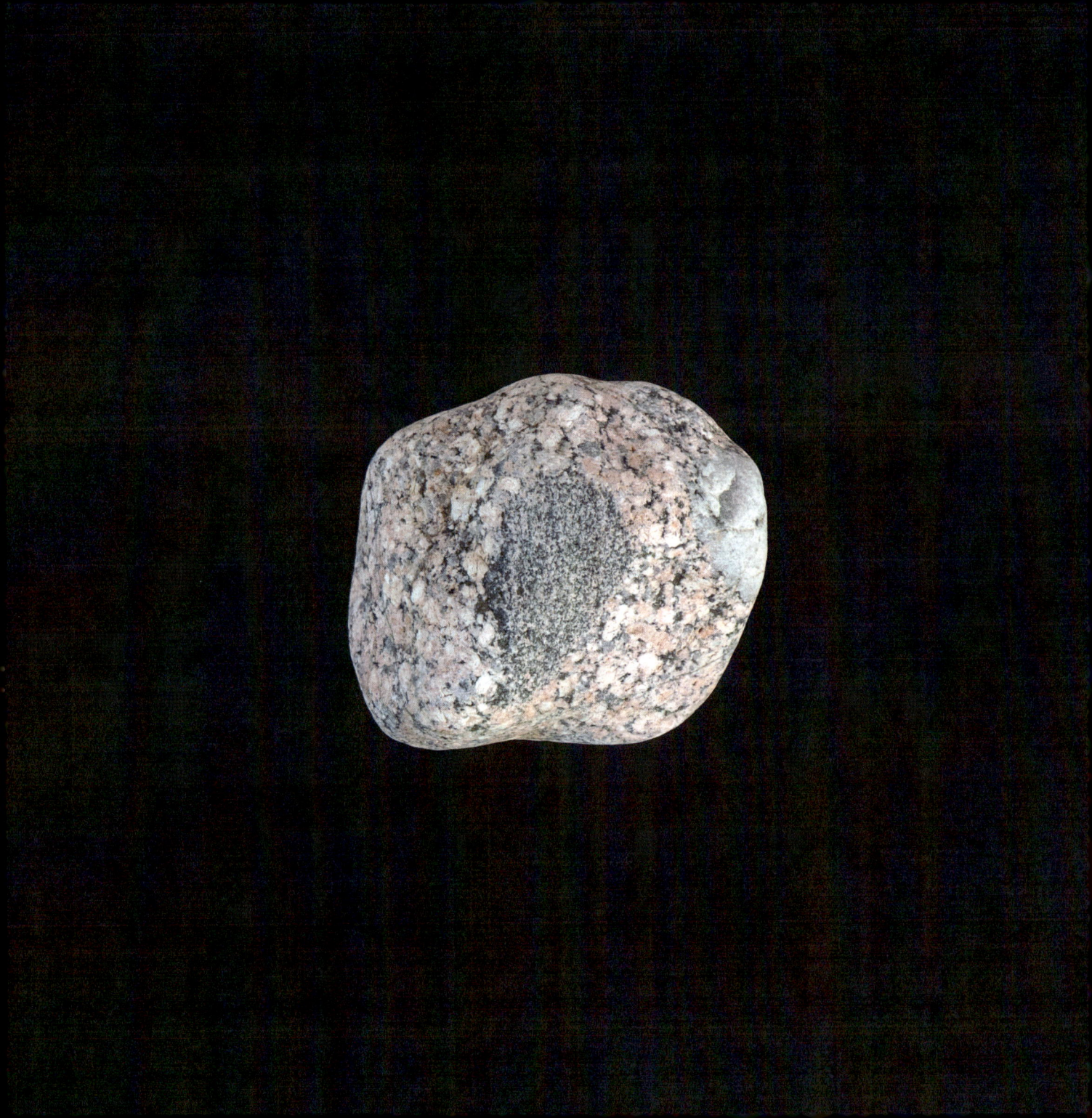

xenolith

Hello, mitochondrion. There is that day in high school biology when the citric acid cycle comes as clear to me as the ringing of a silver bell and I could have led armies through your works like choreography my body had swallowed in tablet form, an entire library of gesture running itself in a loop, the perfect perpetual motion machine, no memorization required. I learned your secret recipe for adenosine triphosphate, donated by a random bacterium who only wanted to hitch a ride in return. What powers the fire ants and black bears, the grasshoppers that r-p-o-p-h-e-s-s-a-g-r'ed off the page in English class where yes we were reading small ee mister cummings and listening to our teacher's Simon & Garfunkel records, feeling our imaginations tumble and turn over slowly like engines just asking for a little more juice. That force that through the green fuse was driving the flower. I sputtered with desire, facing the mysteries, blissed out and unequipped, wondering if I would ever understand anything. How planetesimals accrue around crystal seeds, ribosomes seek out amino acid beads, diatoms flush the sky with oxygen, clinking their rims like champagne flutes. Mycorrhizal basement circuits sparking away in the moist dark under our feet, lace and threads plugged in, powering the whole shebang with exquisite light. It's enough to make a person kneel down in the street, this light. How any small piece, no matter where it comes from, fits exactly right.

: a foreign inclusion in an igneous rock.

craton

Looking around for a safe place to stand, trying to avoid loose manhole covers, glacial crevasses, and the dark sort of trapdoor that opened under Persephone, you might look no farther than this holy book beneath your feet and its sandy, loamy, cobbly, granitic, aquifer-ridden scriptorium renowned for billion-year-old palimpsests that launched a thousand Ph.D. theses and set the old churchmen on their butts. Consider those slo-mo plate collision comb overs that scrape ocean crust up like rocky road ice cream and dump it in scoops on dry land. Consider those mountaintops, eroding as they rise, dropping scree and rain shadow into the valleys below. You might lie back in a playground swing, late in the day when everyone's at dinner, and listen to finches singing from trees. You might note all the flavors of your neighborhood's political flags, flapping in the restless, apolitical, salt-stung breeze coming in off the bay. You might consider time as a randomly variable metronome, or as a tiny package with no return address delivered expressly into your hands, or as a warm, nearly motionless mineral wave that will cover us some day under a custom-made quilt, melted together like a box of crayons left in the sun. When you climb out of that swing, boots down, and take your next breathless steps on this round world, you might feel welcome for a little while longer, you might feel as if maybe you could stay.

: a part of the earth's crust that has attained stability and has been little deformed for a long time.

a field guide to the rocks

An alphabetical listing of elaborations, digressions, sidebars, and tangents to the preceding texts, along with handy descriptions of the specimens.

ACCRETION HYPOTHESIS

Excerpt from Marcia Bjornerud, *Reading the Rocks: The Autobiography of the Earth*. Elsewhere in her wonderful book, she says this, which I find oddly comforting: "Nothing is unusable waste, and nothing will last forever, at least not in any particular form. Matter resides temporarily in various lodging places, then moves on in new guises." A rewording of James Hutton's famous 1788 address to the Royal Society of Edinburgh, which geologists tend to quote with reverence: "The ruins of an older world are visible in the present structure of our planet, and the strata which now compose our continents have been once beneath the sea, and were formed out of the waste of pre-existing continents." See also Marcia Bjornerud, *Timefulness: How Thinking Like a Geologist Can Help Save the World*, and *Turning to Stone: Discovering the Subtle Wisdom of Rocks*.

Color: Many.
Characteristics: Diverse rock types, diverse roundedness, calcite-rich matrix.
Rock type: Concrete with diverse aggregate rocks embedded.

ALABASTER

My kayak is an original Walden Paddler, early nineties, no longer manufactured. It is 100 percent recycled plastic, 10 feet long, 33 pounds. I can wrestle it into the water myself or use an excellent little two-wheeled cart attached with bungee cords. Purchased for me by my mother the same year she bought cribs for my sisters when they had their first babies. My most prized possession. Not for sale. Step to it and I will fight you.

Color: White, ivory tones.
Characteristics: White and ivory quartz. Not alabaster.
Rock type: Rounded pebble of quartz with at least two generations of quartz veins within.

ALGAL BISCUIT

This could also be taken for a potato, which would call for an entirely different set of ingredients.

Color: Gray, white.
Characteristics: Relatively homogeneous gray rock with flat edge of white quartz (residue of a quartz-filled fracture).
Rock type: Immature gray sandstone with remnant of quartz fracture fill or bedding plane smoothed on one side.

ASTEROID

For my sisters.

Color: Black, white, peach-pink.
Characteristics: Interlocking quartz, feldspar, black mica/amphibole.
Rock type: Igneous granite.

ATMOSPHERE

Any resemblance to that heart-stopping Earthrise photo taken during the Apollo 8 moon loop on Christmas Eve 1968 is entirely intentional.

Color: Blue gray, beige, ivory.
Characteristics: White crystalline masses intermixed with black crystalline masses.
Rock type: Metamorphic gneiss pebble, likely quartz and amphibole.

CONGLOMERATE

Local newspaper journalists have to keep track of damn near everything.

Color: Many.
Characteristics: Amalgam of differently rounded clasts.
Rock type: Conglomerate of red, green, gray clasts in quartz cement.

CRATON

Thirty-five cratons have been identified on earth. They are the oldest, most stable roots of the continents, dating to well over a billion years—and perhaps to nearly 4 billion years. (The age of the earth itself is estimated at 4.543 billion years.) These ages are outside human comprehension but can be estimated via radiogenic isotope geochemistry, whereby regular-sized people use large, expensive machines called mass spectrometers to shoot minuscule beams of ionized rock at a detector. Zircons are important in this process. The North American craton lies between the Appalachian Mountains and the Rocky Mountains and runs up into Canada, where it is called the Canadian Shield.

Color: Red-purple.
Characteristics: Fine grain size.
Rock type: Siltstone, weathered smooth.

DENSITY CURRENT

The first letter I wrote, which led to all the others. A letter of accountability. Fair warning. I was scolding myself, but if the shoe fits, now you know what to do.

Color: Dark gray.
Characteristics: Cavities are likely to be left behind as geometric crystal forms weather out of the material.
Rock type: Igneous basalt.

EARTH TIDE

For Peter Pullman, who was right.

Color: Gray blue, pale gray.
Characteristics: Remnant bedding planes in original material, crosscutting later veins.
Rock type: Metamorphosed siltstone with crosscutting quartz-filled veins.

ERRATIC

There is such a field, in Middletown, Rhode Island, filled with exactly these cattle and swallows.

Color: Medium gray.
Characteristics: Harder than glass.
Rock type: Weathering smoky quartz pebble.

FIRECLAY

My guess is as good as yours, but if you're planning to have a conversation with the gods, you need to bring it.

Color: Red, white, gray.
Characteristics: Porous clay matrix.
Rock type: Synthetic brick.

FISSURE VEIN

For Steve, always. Excerpt from Samuel Franklin Emmons (1841-1911), a founding member and president of the Colorado Scientific Society. His paper "On the Origin of Fissure Veins" was published in volume 2 of the *Society's Proceedings* in 1886. I found it digitized by Google via the original book at Harvard University. Emmons also cofounded the Geological Society of America. Two mountains, a glacier, a mineral, and a fossil plant are named after him.

Color: Red, white, black, pink.
Characteristics: Rough-edged sandstone with prominent ~12 mm thick quartz vein, some black staining (Mn mineral?).
Rock type: Metamorphosed sandstone with filled fracture.

FOLIATION

Even rocks need self-care. Maybe especially rocks.

Color: Black, white, peach-pink.
Characteristics: Dark minerals (prominent biotite or black mica) aligned in bands.
Rock type: Metamorphic gneiss.

FOSSIL

Here is where I recount the story of seeing Diane Morra alight from an elevator as I waited for my interview at Worth Publishers, midtown Manhattan, 1979. She was *wearing sneakers.* Great, I thought. I can handle this place.

Color: White, gray, amber.
Characteristics: Crosscutting veins near contact.
Rock type: Two rocks at a prominent contact: at bottom, white siltstone crosscut by strong quartz veins that are weathering out of the rest of the material; at top, quartz-cemented conglomerate of diverse clast types. Not a fossil.

GEOLOGIC RECORD

I could define all the terms in this abecedarian, but that would deprive you of the pleasure of looking them up yourself. If you've read this far, though, you might appreciate knowing good ones I had to leave out: extinction direction, gypsum flower, inverted plunge, kink fold, meteoric water, overbank deposit, pebble armor, residual gravity, wind shadow. There are more.

Color: Medium gray, white.
Characteristics: Quartz and graphite.
Rock type: Metamorphic rock, quartz-graphite schist.

GLACIER TONGUE

Excerpt from William E. Glassley's delightful book *A Wilder Time: Notes from a Geologist at the Edge of the Greenland Ice*, which describes his seasons of research there. On this day: an ice wall cracking off a glacier. Testify.

Color: Many.
Characteristics: Amalgam of differently rounded clasts.
Rock type: Conglomerate of differently weathering clasts in quartz-rich matrix.

GRANITE

An intrusive igneous rock, which means it forms from magma cooling and crystallizing slowly deep underground. Granite doesn't come from lava. It never sees the light of day until the rock around it erodes away or humans come along and blast it out of quarries. It is plutonic—it grows inside the earth's crust. Down there in the crowded underworld with Pluto himself. So granite *is the dragon*.

Color: Pink, white, gray, black.
Characteristics: Interlocking grains.
Rock type: Granite.

GRANULAR DISINTEGRATION

In which I apply for a monastic cell from the anima mundi.

Color: Gray, white.
Characteristics: Sandstone, dark banding.
Rock type: Sandstone, prominent lithic fragments
in quartz cement.

GRATICULE

Boulders from the glacial field in Lincoln Woods State Park, in Lincoln, Rhode Island. Two hand-drawn maps of note:

Map 1. Conor Phalen's map of Lincoln Woods bouldering sites, which I discovered on the Mountain Project website and used as a guide to find them all, an obsession that began in March 2018 and is ongoing. I kept Phalen's map folded up in my wallet and pulled it out whenever I went to visit the boulders. Later, at home, I'd write a letter to the boulders. I was abetted in this boulder obsession by my nephew Travis Soares, who was on his way to becoming an accomplished trail runner and mountain athlete, and who practiced his climbing skills on them. From my 3-10-18 letter: *Travis tells me that Druid's Circle is his favorite place in the park, and I see why. You get the feeling of being among minds. One boulder has a wide vein of what looks like quartz running through it. Beautiful. I wander around and take more pictures. I imagine this place at night with a small campfire lit. I talk to the rocks a bit, with some shyness. I find a clutch of brown chrysalises stuck in a crevice. Despite my stupid office shoes and my camera straps and overloaded coat pockets, I climb up the side of a boulder and look around from up there. I don't have any real words, but I hope I will. Then I climb down.*

Map 2. Sidney S. Rider's "Map of the Colony of Rhode Island—Giving the Indian Names of Locations and the Locations of Great Events in Indian History with Present Political Divisions Indicated," 1903. (A digital copy of this impressive map is available from Yale's Beinecke Rare Book and Manuscript Library here: https://collections.library.yale.edu/catalog/15827688.) Lincoln Woods was purchased by the state of Rhode Island from local property owners and set apart as parkland starting in 1909, but obviously it was home for people for thousands of years prior to colonial invasion in the 1600s. Rider's map shows the park is situated where the Narragansett and Wampanoag lands meet. Quinsnaket, Nipsachuck, Amataconet, Loquassuck. I learn the original name for this place: Caucaunjaivatchuck. The people who called it this would have known these boulders and surely been climbers of them.

Color: Putty, white.
Characteristics: Crosscutting quartz veins.
Rock type: Oblong rounded pebble of siltstone crosscut with late-stage white quartz vein fillings.

GREENSTONE

Sometimes love really is enough.

Color: Medium yellow green.
Characteristics: Harder than glass, zones of weakness/enhanced weathering.
Rock type: Weathered quartz-rich pebble.

LAW OF ORIGINAL HORIZONTALITY

The three other foundational laws of geology are the law of superposition, the law of cross-cutting relationships, and the law of lateral continuity. There's also the concept of unconformity, which involves wizardry. Unconformities are gaps in the geologic record. Excised pages. Geologists regard unconformities as evidence of missing time. Which is real science but sounds a little woo-woo. See the letter for uniformitarianism.

Color: Purple-red, white.
Characteristics: Fine grained, faint layering.
Rock type: Metamorphic red quartzite with subtle bands of clear quartz (few mm diameter) along old bedding planes.

MEANDER SCROLL

Excerpt from Robert Moor, *On Trails: An Exploration*. The earlier part of this quote reads: "Life is a continual struggle to make sense of the world's complexity. Knowledge is hard won, and so both spoken language and writing are ways of fixing and transmitting it. Though we tend to imagine that there is a sharp dichotomy between oral cultures and those that have developed written language, as trail signs reveal, there is a vast array of media—twigs, cairns, drawings, maps—that blur the line between the two."

Color: White, pale taupe.
Characteristics: Rounded mass cut across with multiple generations of fractures and fracture fill.
Rock type: Heavily weathered igneous rock crosscut by white quartz veins.

MÉLANGE

Excerpt from John McPhee, *Assembling California*. According to my notes, he goes to Macedonia with Eldridge Moores to look at ophiolites. Then he goes to California to look at the Franciscan mélange, which geologists originally thought must have slid off the Sierras and collected there in a god-awful pile but now realize was probably scraped off an underthrusting oceanic plate and stuck up onto land over a gazillion years. So you have pieces of the seafloor and the actual mantle sitting on top of the continental crust. Yeah, that.

Color: Red, brown, white, gray.
Characteristics: Multiple rounded clasts, quartz cement
Rock type: Conglomerate with diverse pebble types, well cemented.

MUSICAL SAND

Even an imagined audience with Calliope carries an epiphany.

Color: Red-purple, gray, white.
Characteristics: Poorly sorted sandstone.
Rock type: Sandstone with variable grain size from silt to gravels, all well cemented and weathered smooth.

NUNATAK

The magnetosphere: "the confines of the earth's magnetic field, modified by influence of the solar wind." The front end of the magnetosphere is called the bow shock. The rear is called the magnetotail. Count your lucky stars and bless all that heaving molten iron at the core of the earth. Without the magnetosphere, we would be toast.

Color: Gray, white, brown, yellow.
Characteristics: Plane across sample likely transmitted water, an agent of oxidative weathering, causing rust staining.
Rock type: Fine grained white granite with a fracture across the sample, along which oxygen-rich water flowed.

OROGENY

For context, see the letter for alabaster.

Color: Blue green, gray, white.
Characteristics: Multiple rock types connected by granitic material, possible inclusions.
Rock type: Older gray rock surrounded by younger felsic melt, all of which has weathered and selectively eroded.

PANGAEA

Alluding with the humblest of bows to Anne Sexton's book of transformations.

Color: Many diverse rock types.
Characteristics: Diverse roundedness, asphalt-type matrix.
Rock type: Road material.

PATTERNED GROUND

Of course I would want to know what this is. Automatic geometry. Like someone laid a patio in the arctic tundra. Circles of stones sorted by size. Striped and stepped soil. All you need to do is stand there and watch for a few decades or millennia while frost heaves make all the art. Sources are: Peter D. Kramer, *Listening to Prozac*; Margaret Cheney, *Tesla, Man Out of Time;* Richard Rhodes, *The Making of the Atomic Bomb*; Jeremy Campbell, *Grammatical Man*; Walter Benjamin, *Illuminations*; Peter T. Turley, *Peirce's Cosmology*; Raymond Flood & Michael Lockwood, *The Nature of Time*; Lydia Maria Child, *Hobomok & Other Writings on Indians*; Daniel Halpern, ed., *The Art of the Tale*; Chang Chung-juan, *Creativity and Taoism*; Leslie Marmon Silko, *Ceremony*; Plato, *Euthyphro*; Otto R. Frisch, *The Nature of Matter*.

Color: Red, pale gray to white.
Characteristics: Red feldspars in quartz matrix.
Rock type: Weathered cobble of igneous rock made up of vivid red feldspar and quartz.

PHENOCRYST

Cosmos sulphureus "Cosmic Orange," to be specific. The blooms are plentiful and the seeds are easy to harvest. Once you sow it, you'll have more than enough seeds to give to every gardener in your neighborhood.

Color: Gray, white.
Characteristics: Multiple sizes of crystals in fine matrix.
Rock type: Porphyritic mafic rock.

PLATE TECTONICS

And then he spent the next two months deliriously happy, as if released from bondage, and eventually someone else hired him and it's working out so far. The fairytale that is modern capitalism continues to produce its hypnotic effect on our brains.

Color: White, pink, red.
Characteristics: Heavily weathered siltstone pebble.
Rock type: Sedimentary siltstone.

SANDSTONE

The sand is moving, and so is everything built on it. Coastal armoring or managed retreat? That seems to be the choice. For a good overview on coastal erosion in Rhode Island, see this story by Frank Carini at ecoRI News from May 2021: https://ecori.org/2021-3-18-mother-nature-and-humans-do-battle-along-rhode-islands-coast.

Color: Gray to white.
Characteristics: Cemented grains.
Rock type: Immature sandstone, quartz matrix.

SEDIMENTATION

I was reading about stratigraphy. How geologists mentally untwist, delaminate, and relink layers that have been crosscut, flipped over, half-melted, eroded away, to decode the bedrock. To read the strata, you have to be good at patterns. You need to run past dead ends. You must believe, deep inside every cell in your body, that sense can be made of the mess. Because sense existed at some point. So I could do stratigraphy too. On my living room bookshelf. Turn the stack back to its original horizontal orientation, open each unit to the first line, collect it, repeat. Mix with water and stir until the sediment deposits. Lithify. Make a rock. Sources are: Albert Hofstadter, *Truth and Art*; Karl von Frisch, *Bees: Their Vision, Chemical Senses, and Language*; William Irwin Thompson, ed., *Gaia: A Way of Knowing*; Sandra Harding, *The Science Question in Feminism*; Alison Leadley Brown, *Ecology of Fresh Water*; Wylie Sypher, *Literature and Technology: The Alien Vision*; Elisabeth Kubler-Ross, *On Life After Death*; Annie Dillard, *Teaching a Stone to Talk*; Virginia Woolf, *Three Guineas*; J. Bronowski, *Science and Human Values*; Gretel Ehrlich, *The Solace of Open Spaces*; Wassily Kandinsky, *Sounds*.

Color: Red, brown, taupe, white.
Characteristics: Layering.
Rock type: Well-cemented sandstone with fine interbeds of redder, clay-rich material.

SELENOLOGY

A love story. Excerpt from Robert M. Hazen, *The Story of Earth: The First 4.5 Billion Years, from Stardust to Living Planet.*

Color: White, ivory, gray, pale brown.
Characteristics: White granite with white mica and smoothed feldspars, beautiful piece of metamorphosed sedimentary rock. (Possibly Rhode Island Formation.)
Rock type: Granite cobble that incorporated older sedimentary rock (note cubic cavities, likely held pyrite cubes previously), well smoothed by weathering and erosion.

SHOCK METAMORPHISM

A syllabus.

Color: White, gray, brown.
Characteristics: Pervasive chaotic black mica flakes, few weathering red garnets.
Rock type: Metamorphic schist with garnets indicating high metamorphic grade—white face is quartz dominated, likely an old quartz-filled fracture that hugged the schist, and all is weathered smooth.

SPLENDENT LUSTER

My planet factory is Allin's Cove, a small saltwater estuary located in Barrington, Rhode Island, just south of the opening to Bullocks Cove on Narragansett Bay. In the spring and summer of 2020, after the pandemic hit the globe with full malignancy and we were all sent home to work via zoom in our yoga pants, I walked over to Allin's Cove every day. It's a quick jaunt from where I live in Riverside: along the East Bay Bike Path, through the Bay Spring neighborhood, and down an overgrown path of Japanese knotweed to a stony beach. The cove has been through a lot. Years of effluent from the Rhode Island Lace Works and other manufacturers upstream on Annawamscutt Brook laid sediments of dyes and heavy metals in the mud. In the late fifties, the U.S. Army Corps of Engineers filled part of the cove with material dredged out of the boat channels in Bullocks Cove. They came back much later to fix the terrible erosion this caused and to restore the marsh. They planted native grasses, moved the tidal channel, and built a huge sand spit. This might have been what made all the magic rocks appear. All I know is they were lying there ready for me to jam into my pockets and carry home when I needed them most. Every specimen in this book is from the beach off Byway Road.

Color: Red, white.
Characteristics: Harder than glass.
Rock type: Red quartz pebble shot through with white quartz vein fillings, all rounded by weathering.

STRINGER

So gimp? Check this out. Turns out the knotting craft that uses gimp thread is called scoubidou and started in France in the 1950s. It was named after the hit song "Scoubidou," popularized by French singer Sacha Distel, which was a ripoff of the original song "Apples, Peaches, and Cherries," written by Lewis Allan aka Abel Meeropol (yes, that Abel Meeropol) and sung by Peggy Lee. Backed by a male chorus going "scooby-dooby-scoo-doo." So I wondered, hey does that weird cartoon show for kids Scooby-Doo on American TV in the seventies have anything to do with this? Well. They claim they named the dog after Frank Sinatra's riff "doo-be-doo-be-doo" at the end of "Strangers in the Night." But what is more likely? I think another look at this is called for. I had five Wikipedia tabs and two You Tube pages open at the same time just to get this far. See the letter for sandstone.

Color: Red, white.
Characteristics: Grain size gradation from top to bottom of sample, mineral vein is white quartz.
Rock type: Metamorphosed clayey sandstone with subtle white quartz fracture fill.

SUBDUCTION

How it went: I was a swimmer, and these were the days before waterproof mascara. So I looked like a raccoon for a while and then came to my senses.

Color: White, gray, yellow, brown.
Characteristics: Harder than glass, impressions of lost crystals and surrounding rock fabric.
Rock type: Quartz vein filling that has outlasted its surrounding rock matrix.

TARN

Lakes of the Clouds can loosely be called tarns but not technically. They are not part of a glacial cirque. On the other side of Mount Washington, the famous Tuckerman Ravine is a true cirque (among others in the Presidential Range), and it has an accompanying real tarn called Hermit Lake. What is cool is that Lakes of the Clouds, way up there in the saddle between Mount Washington and Mount Monroe, are spring-fed. Their waters, lifted also by snowmelt and rainfall, are the source of the Ammonoosuc River, which flows 55 miles to the west and eventually joins the mighty Connecticut. I can share all these facts thanks to generous assistance from Dr. Peter Crane, curator of the Gladys Brooks Memorial Library at the Mount Washington Observatory. According to Dr. Crane, the Lakes are thought to be the highest bodies of water in the eastern United States. He was kind enough to send me links to useful source material on glaciers and cirques, which is how I found out about an organization called Friends of the Pleistocene, founded in 1934 and still going strong. You can read about their field trips at www.fop.cascadiageo.org. Also, they have a songbook.

Color: White, gray.
Characteristics: Multiple small, rounded pebbles in quartz-rich matrix.
Rock type: Conglomerate/metamorphosed conglomerate.

TEPHRA

Purloined radio commentary. Red Sox v. Orioles, August 13, 2021. Early innings. Sox win 8-1. Oh, and this is not actually tephra. But it is basalt. So even though it looks like a lopsided baseball that's seen its share of muddy sandlots and flown through the air a lot, it probably just got squeezed out of the earth somewhere really deep underwater.

Color: Dark gray, purple.
Characteristics: Cavities are likely to be left behind as geometric crystal forms weather out of the material.
Rock type: Gray porphyritic basalt with a second (more purple) magma type intermingled.

THERMOKARST TOPOGRAPHY

My goodness, excuse me. Blew right past that trigger warning. See the letter for shock metamorphism.

Color: Gray, tan, white.
Characteristics: Weathered sandstone.
Rock type: Weathered sandstone with quartz fracture fill evident on edges, some recessed areas show lost fracture fill (already weathered out).

TREMOR

I have a dystonic tremor. Or it might be something they call essential tremor. My head tends to shake in a no-no movement. Is it neuromuscular confusion and brain glitch or an appropriate response to all the crap going on out here? It's rare. People take drugs with unfortunate side effects, undergo injections of botulism toxin, or try deep brain stimulation. The latter sounded like it might be kind of nice, almost like a spa treatment, but when I found out they leave the electrodes in, that was a deal breaker.

Color: Gray, pale brown.
Characteristics: Remnant bedding planes have lost fill material, causing recession.
Rock type: Sedimentary rock, small pebbles in silty material, cemented by quartz; likely metamorphosed after lithification.

UNIFORMITARIANISM

Prices have gone up since I wrote this letter, so now I need to take five bucks with me.

Color: White, tan, black.
Characteristics: Plagioclase and feldspars visible.
Rock type: Rounded weathered granite.

VENUS

Paleolithic Europe. Investigate also the Minoan Snake Goddess, Cyclades figurines, Cypriot bird-headed female statues with prominent pubic triangle, Middle Elamite goddesses presenting their breasts with both hands, Mesopotamian bas relief of winged Inanna with talons for feet, standing on the backs of two lions and tightly holding on to her tools, with a pair of owls by her side.

Color: Gray, white.
Characteristics: Rounded pebbles as clasts in quartz matrix.
Rock type: Conglomerate.

WORLD RIFT SYSTEM

Rubric and scoring methodology for this game not included.

Color: Buff, white.
Characteristics: White sandstone with mineral-filled fractures and sandy inclusion.
Rock type: Sandstone or metasandstone.

XENOLITH

Greek "mitos" (thread) + "khondros" (granule). Google electron micrograph portraits of mitochondria. Always invite the traveler in.

Color: Pink, gray, white.
Characteristics: Quartz inclusion, gray inclusion, granitic melt.
Rock type: Granite with two inclusions: white quartz pebble, partly resorbed country rock.

acknowledgments

O yes my rocks are beautiful, but what kind of rocks are they? To find out, I knew I would need the help of a geologist. I never dreamed I would have help from two. Professors Dawn Cardace and Beth Laliberte, faculty members at the University of Rhode Island's Department of Geosciences, generously shared their expertise and turned my pile of rocks into a teaching opportunity: Dawn assigned the students in her Spring 2023 petrology lab the task of identifying them. So, one day in mid-February, I packed all 45 rocks into a rolling suitcase, drove to campus, and handed them over. Dawn's students spent an afternoon examining the specimens, recording ideas, and making sketches. I am delighted to thank the URI geosciences students who explored my rocks in their lab. The results of their observational, nondestructive studies are featured in the field guide section of this book.

I also owe a debt of gratitude to Erin Twomey-Wilson for lending me her undergrad geology reference works, which, it seems, I will never return. One of them, *Dictionary of Geological Terms*, Third Edition, prepared by the American Geological Institute, was my source for the titles and italicized definitions on each page.

I have the great pleasure of thanking photographer and book designer Mike Grinley, who invited all my rocks to sit for their portraits in his cozy studio in the woods of western Massachusetts. His collaborative spirit has been a cornerstone.

I am grateful to Beth Donovan, Martha Donovan, and Maya Janson for being pillars of encouragement, to Walker Rumble for enduring rock piles everywhere in the house, and to our gorgeous planet for making all the art.

Thank you to Wet Cement Press for laying a foundation that supports experiment. Many thanks also to the editors of the following journals for publishing these pieces:

—"granular disintegration," "fissure vein," "accretion hypothesis," "phenocryst," "musical sand," and "craton" in *Tupelo Quarterly*, January 2025.

—"splendent luster," "greenstone," "sandstone," and "nunatak" in the anthology *Dreaming Awake: New Contemporary Prose Poetry from the United States, Australia, and the United Kingdom* (MadHat Press, 2023).

—"granite," "earth tide," and "atmosphere," *The Citron Review*, October 2023.

—"tremor," **82 Review 10.2* (2022).

—"alabaster," "asteroid," "tarn," "algal biscuit," and "conglomerate," *Sweet 14.2* (2022).

Thank you to the following publishers for permission to reprint the epigraphs and quotes used in this book:

about the author

Karen Donovan's latest book of poems, *Monad+Monadnock*, was published by Wet Cement Press in 2022. She is also the author of *Planet Parable*, which was published by Etruscan Press in an innovative multi-author volume called *Trio*. Her other collections of poems are *Your Enzymes Are Calling the Ancients* (Persea Books), which won the Lexi Rudnitsky / Editor's Choice Award, and *Fugitive Red* (University of Massachusetts Press), which won the Juniper Prize. Her book of illustrated short prose, *Aard-vark to Axolotl* (Etruscan Press), is a collection of tiny stories and essays inspired by the engravings in a vintage Webster's dictionary. From 1985 to 2005 she co-edited ¶: A Magazine of Paragraphs, a print journal of very short prose. She lives in Rhode Island, way too close to the water.

www.ingramcontent.com/pod-product-compliance
Lightning Source LLC
Chambersburg PA
CBRC090843120626
46551CB00009B/741